# THE DIANA YEARS

People weekly

**EDITOR-IN-CHIEF** Norman Pearlstine
**EDITORIAL DIRECTOR** Henry Muller
**EDITOR OF NEW MEDIA** Daniel Okrent

**CHAIRMAN, CEO** Don Logan
**EXECUTIVE VICE PRESIDENTS** Elizabeth Valk Long, Jim Nelson, Joseph A. Ripp

**MANAGING EDITOR** Carol Wallace
**EXECUTIVE EDITORS** Cutler Durkee, Susan Toepfer
**ASSISTANT MANAGING EDITORS** Ross Drake, Charles Leerhsen, Joe Treen (Administration), Carey Winfrey, Roger R. Wolmuth, Jacob Young (Development)
**EDITOR, SPECIAL PROJECTS** Eric Levin
**NEWS DIRECTOR** Kristen Kelch
**SENIOR EDITORS** Max Alexander, Jack Friedman, Susan Hornik, Robert F. Howe, Bonnie Johnson, James C. Katz, Jack Kelley (Los Angeles), Janice Min, Ralph Novak, Joseph Poindexter, Elizabeth Sporkin
**ART DIRECTOR** John Shecut Jr.
**PICTURE EDITOR** Maura Foley
**CHIEF OF REPORTERS** Nancy Pierce Williamson
**CHIEF OF STAFF** Sarah Brody Janover
**ASSOCIATE EDITORS** Peter Castro, Kim Cunningham, Thomas Fields-Meyer, Michelle Green, Kim Hubbard, Michael A. Lipton, William Plummer, J.D. Reed, Leah Rozen, Karen S. Schneider
**SENIOR WRITERS** Peter Ames Carlin, Steven Dougherty, Alec Foege, Bruce Frankel, Tom Gliatto, Bill Hewitt, Richard Jerome, Pam Lambert, Steven Lang, Michael J. Neill, Curtis Rist, Patrick Rogers, Cynthia Sanz, Susan Schindehette, Alex Tresniowski
**STAFF WRITERS** Chuck Arnold, Nick Charles, Sophfronia Scott Gregory, Dan Jewel, Samantha Miller, Anne-Marie O'Neill, Lisa Russell, Kyle Smith, Joyce Wansley
**WRITER-REPORTERS** Andrew Abrahams (Deputy Chief), Veronica Burns, Denise Lynch (Deputies, Special Projects), Lisa Kay Greissinger, Mary S. Huzinec, Toby Kahn, Sabrina McFarland, Irene Kubota Neves, Maria Speidel
**REPORTERS** Greg Adkins, Marilyn Anderson, Amy Brooks, Jennifer Chrebet, David Cobb Craig, Rebecca Dameron, Amalia Duarte, Deirdre Gallagher, Mary Green, Ann Guerin, Jeremy Helligar, Jason Lynch, Hugh McCarten, Erik Meers, Lan N. Nguyen, Gail Nussbaum, Vincent R. Peterson, Marisa Sandora, Mary Shaughnessy, Ying Sita, Brooke Bizzell Stachyra, Leslie Strauss, Jane Sugden, Randy Vest, Robin Ward
**RESEARCH OPERATIONS** James Oberman (Manager), Robert Britton, Steven Cook, Suzy Im, Celine Wojtala
**PICTURE DEPARTMENT** Beth Filler (Deputy), Maddy Miller (Deputy, Special Projects), Mary Fanette, Holly Holden, Denise Straga, Ann Tortorelli (Associate Editors), Suzanne Cheruk, Lisa Morris, Josef Siegle, Eileen Sweet, John Toolan, Freyda Tavin, Mindy Viola, Blanche Williamson (Assistant Editors), Stan J. Williams (Picture Desk), Michael Brandson, Tom Mattie; Karin Grant, Michele Stueven (Los Angeles), Kristy Jell (London)
**ART DEPARTMENT** Hilli Pitzer (Deputy Director), Phil Simone (Special Projects Director), Helene Elek, Janice Hogan (Associate Directors), Angela Alleyne, Gregory Monfries (Assistant Directors), Tom Allison, Ronnie Brandwein Keats, Michelle Angelee Smith (Designers), Allan D. Bintliff Sr., Nora Cassar, Charles Castilio, Brien Foy, Stephen Pabarue, Joseph Randazzo
**COPY DESK** Patricia R. Kornberg (Chief), Will Becker (Deputy), Judith I. Fogarty, Ben Harte, Rose Kaplan (Copy Coordinators), Hollis C. Bernard, Linda Crawford, William Doares, Alan Levine, Mary C. Radich, Muriel C. Rosenblum, Joanann Scali, Sheryl F. Stein (Copy Editors), Lillian Nici, Deborah Ratel, Patricia Rommeney (Assistants)
**OPERATIONS** Alan Anuskiewicz (Manager), Liz Zale (Deputy), Michael G. Aponte, Donna Cheng, Denise M. Doran, Erikka V. Haa, George W. Hill, Michelle Lockhart, Key Martin, Ali Namvar, Helen Russell, Ellen Shapiro, Larry Whiteford
**TECHNOLOGY** Eric Mischel (Director), Esther Chang, Scott Damm, Pablo Figueroa, Thomas Fitzgibbon, Janine Gordon, Fred Kao, Cheroc Lawless, Gregory Paik, Alison Sawyer, Davina Tang, Barry Wolborsky
**PRODUCTION** Robert Bronzo, Paul Castrataro, Geri Flanagan, Lizann Nagel Fragiotta, Paul Zelinski (Managers), Catherine Barron, David Pandy, Susan Popler-Roy, Kathleen Seery, Anthony White
**IMAGING** Betsy Castillo (Manager), Willis Caster Jr. (Assistant Manager), Warren Thompson (Supervisor), Steven Cadicamo, Paul Dovell, Robert Fagan, Francis Fitzgerald, Fitzgerald Gordon, Kevin Grimstead, Henry Groskinsky, James M. Lello, Brian Luckey, Anthony G. Moore, Craig Puffer, Joanne Recca, Robert Roszkowski, Randall Swift, Peter Tylus, Victor Van Carpels, Susan Vroom
**DIRECTOR, NEW MEDIA** Hala Makowska
**NEW MEDIA DEPARTMENT** Dylan Jones (Editor, PEOPLE Online), Heather Craig, Lorraine Goods, Heather White (Picture Editor)
**PUBLIC AFFAIRS** Susan Ollinick (Director), Dianne Jones, Sheri Lapidus, Marie L. Parker
**EDITORIAL BUSINESS MANAGER** David Geithner, Orpha Davis (Deputy), Zena Norbont (Associate)
**ADMINISTRATION** Bernard Acquaye, Isabel Alves, Shelley Bacote, Xiomara D. Cotton, Nancy Eils, Joy Fordyce, Claudette Hutchinson, Barbara Kligman, Samantha McIntyre, Ruth Oden, Mari Parks, Jean Reynolds, Shirley Van Putten, Martha White, Maureen S. Fulton (Letters/Syndication Manager)
**NEWS BUREAU** Sarah Skolnik (Deputy Chief), Liza Hamm, Anna Lisa Raya, William Brzozowski, Richard G. Williams
**NATIONAL CORRESPONDENT:** Giovanna Breu
**DOMESTIC BUREAUS CHICAGO**, Cindy Dampier (Chief), Luchina Fisher, Joanne Fowler Lorna Grisby, Leisa Marthaler; **HOUSTON**, Anne Maier (Chief), Donna Buchala; **LOS ANGELES**, Todd Gold (Deputy Chief), Craig Tomashoff (Associate Chief), Ken Baker, Lorenzo Benet, Karen Brailsford, Thomas Cunneff, Johnny Dodd, John Hannah, Elizabeth Leonard, Danielle Morton, Vicki Sheff-Cahan, Lyndon Stambler, Lynda Wright, Paula Yoo, Florence Nishida, Monica Clark, Cecilia de la Paz, Jennifer Harding; **MIAMI**, Meg Grant (Chief), Marisa Salcines, Fannie Weinstein, Leslie Marine; **NEW YORK**, Maria Eftimiades (Acting Chief), Ron Arias, Julia Campbell, Anthony Duignan-Cabrera, Nancy Matsumoto, Elizabeth F. McNeil, Sue Miller, Cynthia Wang, Mercedes Mitchell; **WASHINGTON**, Garry Clifford (Chief), Linda Kramer, Margie Bonnett Sellinger, Vornida Seng, Angela Waters
**EUROPEAN EDITOR** Fred Hauptfuhrer
**EUROPEAN BUREAU** Lydia Denworth (Chief), Bryan Alexander, Nina Biddle, Simon Perry
**SPECIAL CORRESPONDENTS ALBUQUERQUE**, Michael Haederle; **ATLANTA**, Gail Wescott; **BOSTON**, Tom Duffy; **CHICAGO**, Barbara Sandler; **DENVER**, Vickie Bane; **JERUSALEM**, Abe Rabinovich; **LONDON**, Joanna Blonska, Margaret Wright; **LOS ANGELES**, Mitchell Fink, Anne-Marie Otey, Jeff Schnaufer; **MEMPHIS/NASHVILLE**, Jane Sanderson; **MIAMI**, Don Sider; **MINNEAPOLIS**, Margaret Nelson; **PARIS**, Cathy Nolan; **ATHENS**, Toula Vlahou; **SAN ANTONIO**, Joseph Harmes, Bob Stewart; **SALT LAKE CITY**, Cathy Free; **WASHINGTON**, Mary Esselman, Jennifer Mendelsohn, Jane Sims Podesta
**CONTRIBUTING PHOTOGRAPHERS** Harry Benson, Ian Cook, Stephen Ellison, Acey Harper, Steve Kagan, Christopher Little, Jim McHugh, Robin Platzer, Neal Preston, Co Rentmeester, Mark Sennet, Peter Serling, Barry Staver, Dale Wittner, Taro Yamasaki
**TIME INC.**
**EXECUTIVE EDITORS** Joëlle Attinger, José M. Ferrer III
**DEVELOPMENT EDITOR** Isolde Motley
**EDITORIAL SERVICES** Sheldon Czapnik (Director), Claude Boral (General Manager); Thomas E. Hubbard (Photo Lab); Lany Walden McDonald (Research Center); Beth Bencini Zarcone (Picture Collection); Thomas Smith (Technology); James Macove (Marketing); Maryann Kornely (Syndication)
**EDITORIAL TECHNOLOGY** Paul Zazzera (Vice President); Damien Creavin (Director)

**PRESIDENT** Ann S. Moore
**VICE PRESIDENT** Jeremy B. Koch
**CONSUMER MARKETING DIRECTOR** Greg Harris
**BUSINESS MANAGER** Robert D. Jurgrau
**GROUP PRODUCTION DIRECTOR** Tracy T. Windrum
**PRODUCTION DIRECTOR** Thomas C. Colaprico

**PUBLISHER** Nora P. McAniff
**ASSOCIATE PUBLISHER/ADVERTISING** Peter Bauer
**ASSOCIATE PUBLISHER/MARKETING** Vanessa Reed
**ADVERTISING DIRECTOR** John J. Gallagher

**2**

*THE DIANA YEARS*

EDITOR: Eric Levin

ART DIRECTOR: Anthony Kosner

PICTURE EDITORS: Caren Clarke, Lynn Levine, Maddy Miller, Mindy Viola

SENIOR WRITERS: Barbara Kantrowitz, Jill Smolowe

CHIEF OF REPORTERS: Denise Lynch

CONTRIBUTING EDITOR: Richard Burgheim

LONDON CORRESPONDENTS: Lydia Denworth, Margaret Wright

ART ASSISTANTS: Brien Foy, Stephen Pabarue

COPY EDITORS: Ben Harte, Ricki Tarlow

OPERATIONS: Michelle Lockhart

IMAGING: Brian Luckey, Warren Thompson

Special thanks to Angela Alleyne, Tom Allison, Alan Anuskiewicz, Michael G. Aponte, Robert Britton, Betsy Castillo, Steven Cook, Helene Elek, Suzy Im, Patricia R. Kornberg, Louise Lague, Averie LaRussa, James Oberman, Joseph Napolitano, Hilli Pitzer, Susan Power, Cynthia Sanz, Adrienne Sayer, Matthew Semble, Celine Wojtala, Liz Zale, Anthony M. Zarvos and (in London) Joanne Fowler and Jerene Jones

TIME INC. HOME ENTERTAINMENT
MANAGING DIRECTOR: David Gitow
DIRECTOR, CONTINUITIES AND SINGLE SALES: David Arfine
DIRECTOR, CONTINUITIES AND RETENTION: Michael Barrett
DIRECTOR, NEW PRODUCTS: Alicia Longobardo
PRODUCT MANAGERS: Christopher Berzolla, Robert Fox, Stacy Hirschberg, Michael Holahan, Amy Jacobsson, Jennifer McLyman, Dan Melore
MANAGER, RETAIL AND NEW MARKETS: Thomas Mifsud
ASSOCIATE PRODUCT MANAGERS: Louisa Bartle, Alison Ehrmann, Nancy London, Dawn Weland
ASSISTANT PRODUCT MANAGERS: Meredith Shelley, Betty Su
EDITORIAL OPERATIONS DIRECTOR: John Calvano
FULFILLMENT DIRECTOR: Michelle Gudema
FINANCIAL DIRECTOR: Tricia Griffin
ASSOCIATE FINANCIAL MANAGER: Amy Maselli
MARKETING ASSISTANT: Sarah Holmes

CONSUMER MARKETING DIVISION
PRODUCTION DIRECTOR: John E. Tighe
BOOK PRODUCTION MANAGER: Donna Miano-Ferrara
ASSISTANT BOOK PRODUCTION MANAGER: Jessica McGrath

TIME INC. MAGAZINES
EDITOR-IN-CHIEF: Norman Pearlstine
EDITORIAL DIRECTOR: Henry Muller
EDITOR OF NEW MEDIA: Daniel Okrent

TIME INC.
CHAIRMAN, CEO: Don Logan
EXECUTIVE VICE PRESIDENTS: Elizabeth Valk Long, Jim Nelson, Joseph A. Ripp

# THE DIANA YEARS

COMMEMORATIVE EDITION

**SHINING TIME**
**In 1989, Diana positively glowed during a visit to Hong Kong—one of 48 overseas trips she made that year.**

SEA OF LOVE Literally millions of bouquets were placed outside Buckingham and Kensington (here) Palaces.

**T**he death of Princess Diana on August 31, 1997, was one of those rare and terrible events that so jars people that they never forget where they were when they first heard the news. It was inconceivable that the glamour, the goodness and the verve that was Diana could have been erased in an instant. The void left by the remarkable woman whom William, 15, and Harry, 12, called Mummy and British Prime Minister Tony Blair aptly anointed "The People's Princess" was huge. Its true dimensions could only be grasped six days later, when the funeral of the 36-year-old Princess of Wales drew millions of mourners into London's streets and another 2 billion people to their TV sets. The world had lost a patrician with a common touch—a beacon, a magnet and a friend.

**GUARD OF HONOR** Philip, William, Earl Spencer, Harry and Charles walked behind the cortege the last mile of its journey to Westminster Abbey; Harry's roses and card topped his mother's casket.

## FROM THE HEART...
Every moment of the hour-long service was by the book, save one: her younger brother Earl Spencer's eulogy. Standing before "a world in shock," he stunned the assemblage with his passionate tribute to a woman who "needed no royal title to continue to generate her particular brand of magic." With the 1,900 mourners inside the Abbey as his witnesses, he vowed that "we, your blood family, will do all we can" to ensure that Diana's sons would get the sort of "imaginative and loving" upbringing their mother had intended.

## ... AND THE SOUL
Fighting tears, Elton John performed "Candle in the Wind 1997," with the lyrics reworked to honor "England's Rose." As he sang, Prince Harry buried his face in his hands and sobbed.

**D**isbelief and horror at the violence of Diana's untimely death gave way to an unprecedented outpouring of public grief that reverberated around the globe

**POMP AND SAD CIRCUMSTANCE**
The principal male mourners looked on
as Diana's body was placed in a hearse
for the journey to Althorp House,
the Spencers' ancestral home.

**UNIVERSAL GRIEF**
The people who jammed London's
streets to honor Diana's memory
traversed lines of age, race,
sexual orientation and gender.

After the service, Diana's casket made the 75-mile journey from London to her family's 550-acre estate in Northamptonshire, where the princess was quietly buried. At times during the 3½-hour procession, so many bouquets were showered on the hearse as mourners spontaneously applauded that the driver had to use the windshield wipers.

# ABOUT FACE

## Her genius was a gift for projecting mood while preserving mystery

**H**ow many times could we look at that face? Infinitely, it seemed. In 16 years, Diana (at left in her official 21st-birthday portrait, by Snowdon), never lost her power to fascinate. How did she do it? Hers was certainly not a conventional beauty. The nose, for example, was too long and broad. But the generous scale of her smooth features formed a perfect stage for her distinctly and enchantingly unroyal breadth of emotions. Diana was a woman of a thousand expressions, each a tantalizing peek into her soul. She could be bashful or brazen, somber or sultry, poised or playful. Like Garbo and Jackie O., Diana held back part of herself, maintaining the mystery. Perhaps that was the basis of her seduction. She made us think we knew her so well; yet we didn't really know her at all.

## PLAYFUL AND PENSIVE

**The new princess early perfected her "classic Di" look— proper yet flirtatious. In 1985, she met the Pope, rode in a gondola with Charles and continued to establish herself as a woman of the world.**

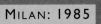

MILAN: 1985

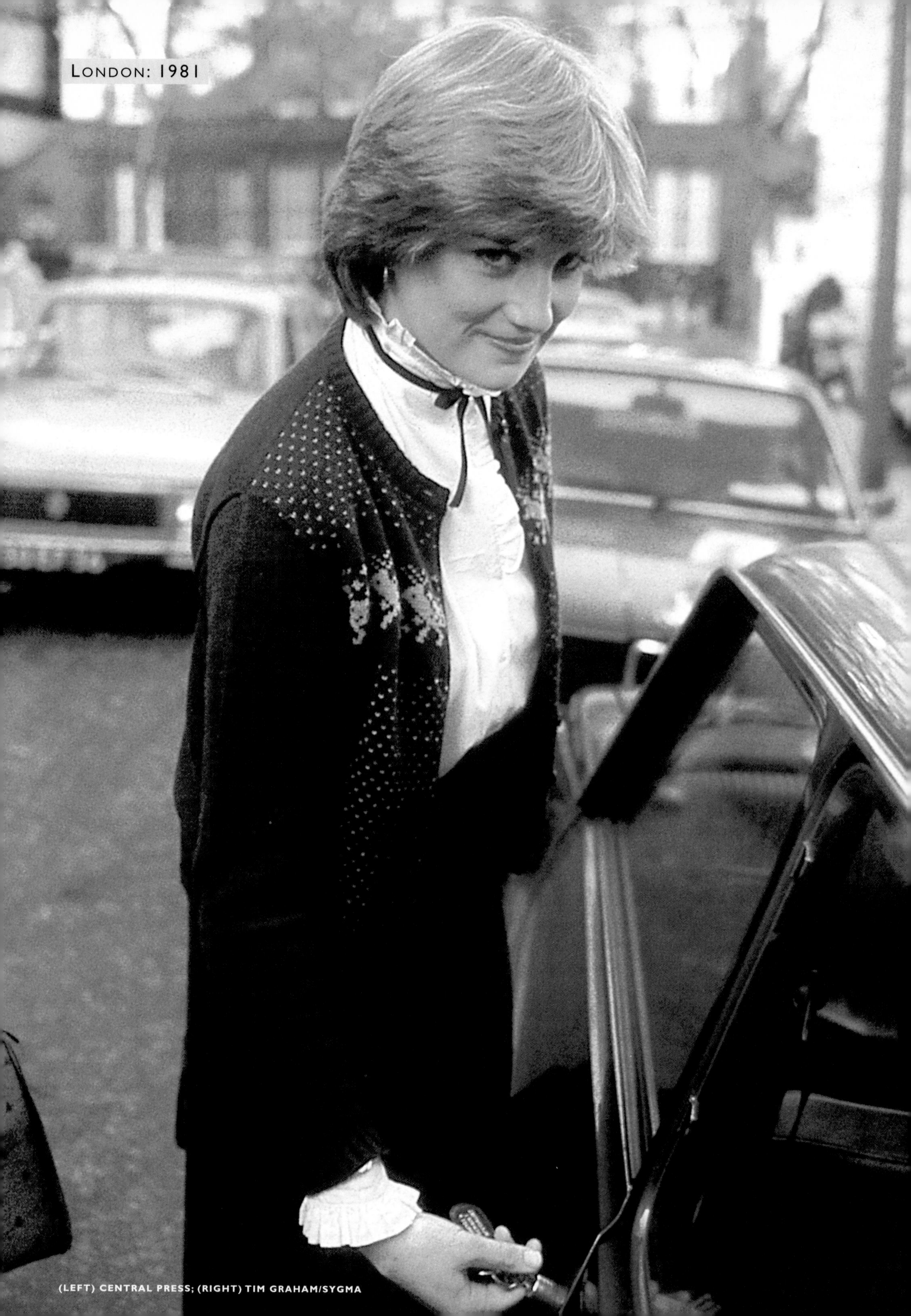


(LEFT) CENTRAL PRESS; (RIGHT) TIM GRAHAM/SYGMA

## KEYS TO THE KINGDOM

—

A few months before her wedding, Lady Diana Spencer left for a weekend trip wearing a girlish cotton blouse and sweater. But as a princess she traveled in style—donning, for example, sapphires, diamonds and the Spencer tiara at a gala in Australia. The miniature of the Queen was a gift from Her Majesty.

—

## BEST ACTRESS

Appearing in a
television documentary
at the Waleses' country
home, Diana tried
hard to hide her
disappointment and
unhappiness over a
marriage that was
already a sham.

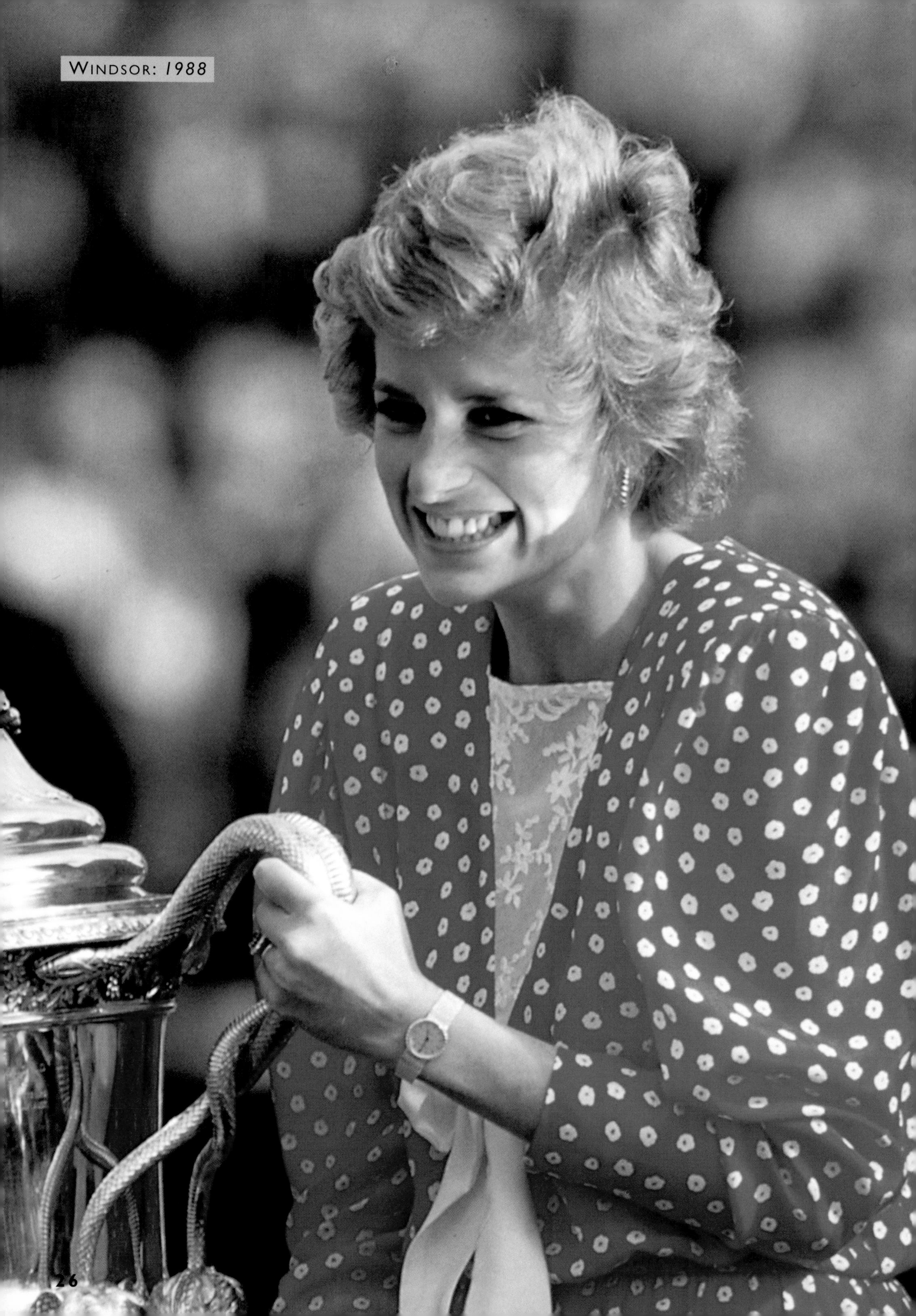

GRIPPING

Whether representing Britain at
a military parade or presenting
a trophy at a polo match,
Diana put her best
face forward.

ITALY: *1985*

(LEFT) DAVID LEVENSON/COLORIFIC–WHEELER PICTURES;
(RIGHT) PHOTOGRAPHERS INTERNATIONAL/OUTLINE PRESS

## COME RAIN, COME SHINE

Whatever the weather—
Highland fog or glint of sun
in the gloaming—at almost any
public function it was easy
to pick out the princess:
She was the one
clutching the bouquet.

ANZIO: *1985*

TIM GRAHAM/SYGMA

## FARAWAY

In the mid-'80s, Diana almost single-headedly made hats fashionable again. But beneath the brim she often seemed pensive and sad—sometimes fittingly so, as on the trip to Italy with Charles, honoring soldiers killed in World War II.

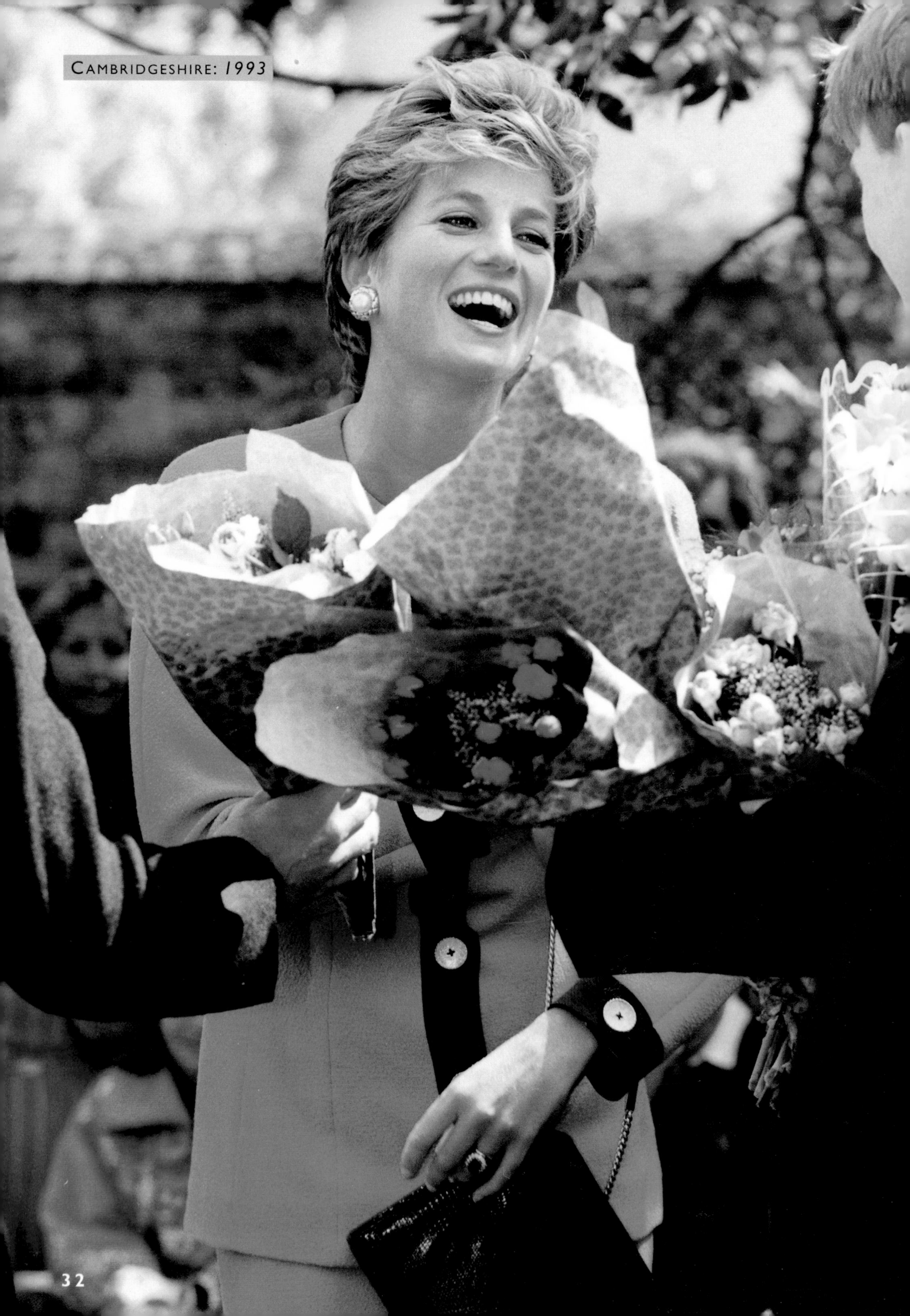

## IN HER ELEMENT

Over the years, Diana grew ever more self-assured in public. Gone by the late '80s was her famously tentative smile. After the 1992 separation, she seemed glad to be on her own.

STAFFORDSHIRE: 1994

## A GEM OF MANY FACETS

—

Diana could appear somber, even forbidding —as she did during ceremonies in Normandy honoring William the Conqueror. But at a polo match a few months earlier, the princess, nearly 27, seemed almost girlish, not too different from the demure nursery school aide who captured a prince.

—

WINDSOR: 1987

## IN MOURNING COLORS

At an Armistice Day ceremony, Diana donned a solemn black hat and veil to review a parade honoring World War I veterans. The observance was on Paris's Champs Elysées, an ironic foreshadowing of her tragic fate.

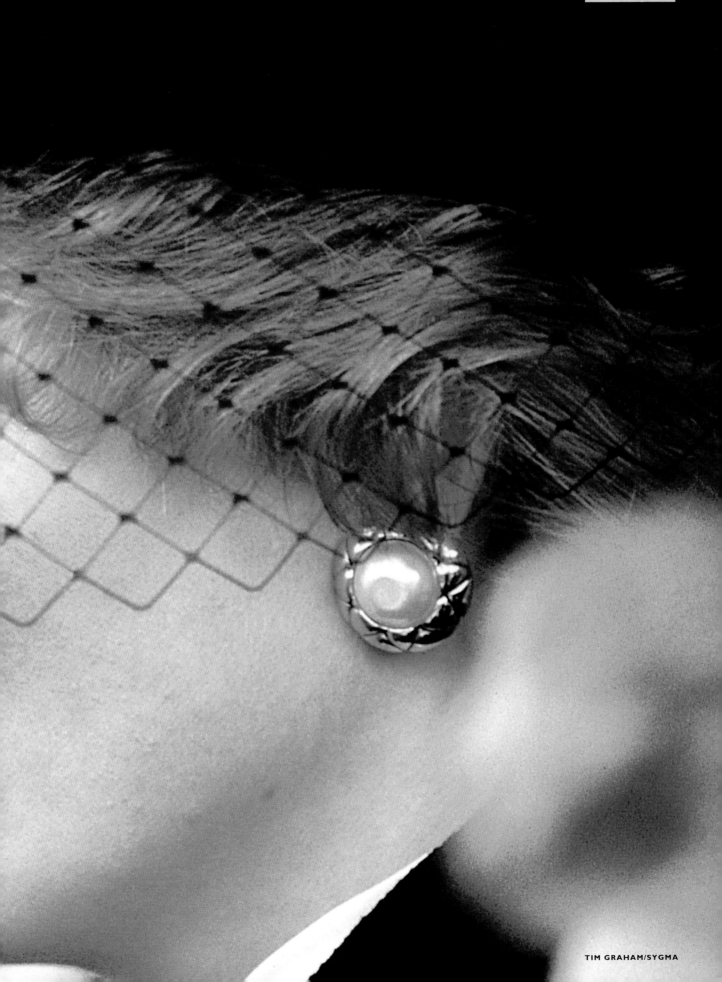

**BLISSFUL**
in their first meeting
with the press after
their postwedding
cruise, Charles and
Diana tenderly held
hands at Balmoral, the
royal family's Scottish
retreat. Diana told
reporters she "highly
recommended" married
life; but in private, the
newlyweds had already
begun arguing about
Charles's continuing
relationship with
Camilla Parker Bowles.

# THE DIANA YEARS

From her Scottish honeymoon
to a hoof with Travolta, the marital Big Chill
and the Christie's auction, these moments
measure the arc of her celebrity and
her world-conquering charm

At 19, when she first blinked for the press, Diana was unsophisticated but nonetheless naturally shrewd—always listening, watching, learning. Bereft of guidance from the royal household, Diana gamely set out to carve a role for herself that went far beyond producing the requisite "heir and a spare." As she redefined royal glamour, championed unchic causes and opened her heart to people the world over, she reshaped the creaky role of princess for a celebrity-worshipping, mass-media age; in the process, she left behind an incomparable album of absorbing images. Though divorce ended Diana's chance of becoming Queen of England, the phenomenal outpouring of grief and affection that attended her death made it evident, to commoner and royal alike, that she'd earned the title she once said she coveted most: Queen of People's Hearts.

**DID YOU** really have to show them to everybody?'' Charles asked his fiancée after her backlit legs made front pages. Diana had hoped that if she posed for photographers besieging the kindergarten where she taught, they would go away. They didn't —right to the tragic end.

# Every detail of Diana's life—from the size of her ring to the size of her shoes—suddenly became public property

**HIS 'N' HERS** The bride said she selected the $42,000 diamond-and-sapphire engagement ring from a proffered tray because "it was the biggest." Later, Charles sent her a Prince of Wales signet to match his own.

# PREGNANT

with William in 1982 (left), Diana looked glum when she and Charles attended the annual Thoroughbred races at Ascot. As a new mother, she suffered postpartum depression and a serious bout of bulimia. Her son (here, at 8 months) was the only joy in her life, she told friends.

# CROWDS

went wild for Diana during the Waleses' first major tour— to Australia in 1983. The outpour stung the prince, heretofore the unrivaled star. While Diana sympathized, she adapted quickly to the spotlight. "You couldn't indulge in feeling sorry for yourself," she later recalled. "You had to either sink or swim. . . . I swam."

## LONELY

but not alone in a walkabout at Ayers Rock during the Australian trip, Charles and Diana were actually surrounded by photographers. Although Diana took along William, then 9 months old, she saw the baby only on weekends. During most of the family's six-week stay, Wills stayed with his nanny on a remote farm while his parents toured the country.

# DANCING

**in Australia in 1985, Charles and Di kept smiling,
though their marriage was deeply troubled.
As Diana said later, "We didn't want to
disappoint the public."**

GUESTS at the White House in 1985, Charles chatted up Nancy Reagan while Diana twirled with John Travolta. Later she waltzed with Clint Eastwood and Neil Diamond.

RANDY TAYLOR/SYGMA

I THINK the biggest disease this world suffers from ... [is] people feeling unloved," said Diana (at a London hospice in 1985). "I can give love.... I'm very happy to do that, and I want to do that."

# BY 1986

**her bulimia was "rampant," recalled
Diana (at a Vienna banquet that year).
"I was crying out for help."**

KEN GOFF

**DURING** their visit to Toronto in 1991, Charles and Diana could not conceal their private estrangement from the public. A year later, Prime Minister John Major announced their official separation.

POSING

solo at the Taj Mahal in 1992, Diana created an indelible image of the neglected wife. Meanwhile, Charles, who had made a premarital vow to someday visit the famous site with his wife, stayed behind in Delhi.

TIM GRAHAM/SYGMA

**IMPASSIVE** as
bookends, Charles and Diana
endured each other at a V-J Day
parade in London in August
1995 as Harry and Wills spoke
volumes with their wrists.

**ENJOYING** her stardom at a 1995 benefit in Manhattan for United Cerebral Palsy, Diana, together with Colin Powell (reportedly her many-times-removed cousin through Spencer ancestors who once lived in Jamaica), received awards from Barbara Walters and Henry Kissinger. Upon her death, Kissinger recalled, "She was a lovely human being with a very wicked sense of humor."

# WORE STORIES What 1,100
bidders paid $3.26 million for at Christie's in New York
City on June 25 (inset) was not only 79 gowns owned
by Diana but the aura of personal and royal history
attached to each. With Christie's chairman Lord
Hindlip, Diana toured the galleries before a preview
party that—combined with ticket and catalog sales
and the auction itself—boosted total proceeds to $5.76
million, all for AIDS and breast-cancer charities.

# ENCOUNTERS

In the last year of her life, Diana lost neither her common touch nor her glamour. In March 1997, she strode into a ballet performance in London. In June, she knelt with children at a Hindu temple in London after receiving a *chandlo*— a traditional Hindu sign of respect for an honored guest.

# SHUTTER

**AT FIRST SIGHT**
Diana enjoyed the
press in March 1981
in Romsey, England.

# BUGGED

## Diana and the paparazzi had a love-hate link to the bitter end

Though she could wield words and good deeds to powerful effect, the world knew Diana primarily through the lens. No one appreciated, or resented, the power of that relentless eye more than Diana herself. When she wanted to send a message, be it a personal one about her marriage or a political one about her causes, she was only too willing to sit for, or orchestrate, a shot. But when the shutter stole moments she never intended to share, she could become viperous. "You make my life hell!" she screamed at a paparazzo in 1993. In her final years, the once Shy Di likened media intrusions to rape, and obtained a restraining order against one pesky photographer. In 1997, Britain passed an anti-stalking law that she hoped would finally afford her some surcease.

# The cameras loved Diana,
## but the feeling was not always mutual

### ENDURANCE TEST
In late 1980, before Diana adapted to the constant press attention, she felt hounded and wept after the picture above was taken. The paparazzi later slipped an apology into her sunroof, launching an alternately affectionate and abusive relationship. Despite round-the-clock efforts (including staking out Coleherne Court, right, where she lived), photographers never snapped the courting couple together until their engagement became public.

**DI SPIED** London gym owner Bryce Taylor sold surreptitious snaps of Diana (like this one, from a ceiling camera) for $187,000 in 1993. Feeling "utterly betrayed," Di sued him and settled out of court. "I'm a product," she once said, "that sells well."

**THE FUGITIVE** Scotland Yard kept Di (code-named Pink Panther) under surveillance in 1994, but that didn't discourage the press (below, as she shopped in London).

# $A$s a single woman without the direct protection of the Palace, Diana struggled to maintain her privacy

—

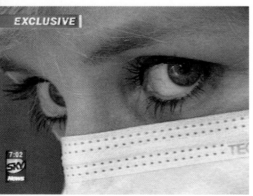

**TELL ALL** Though she was a canny manipulator of the media, Diana professed bewilderment during an interview with the **BBC** in 1995. "I never encouraged the media," she said. "There was a relationship which worked before, but now I can't tolerate it because it's become abusive."

**RAISED EYEBROWS** British critics accused Diana (in surgical mask) of staging a publicity stunt in 1996 when she watched open-heart surgery on a 7-year-old boy from Cameroon in a televised operation at a Middlesex hospital.

**HEATED HEIST**
In London in July 1996, a month before she won an injunction keeping paparazzo Martin Stenning away from her, Diana angrily swiped his motorbike keys. In an affidavit, she admitted that at other times she had retaliated against his abusive language and stalking by grabbing his camera, flash or invoice book (later turning the property over to police).

# ONCE

"Here is the stuff of which fairy tales are made," intoned the Archbishop of Canterbury, perhaps forgetting how scary and dark your average fairy tale can be. No matter, three-quarters of a billion people in 74 countries were right there with him as they tuned in to share the magnificent moment with the 2,650 guests in St. Paul's Cathedral. They weren't disappointed. Every second of the hour-long ceremony seemed perfectly choreographed—from the music (especially Charles's favorite soprano, Kiri Te Kanawa, singing a Handel aria) to the glittering guest list (almost every living royal in the world, including Queen Margrethe II of Denmark, Queen Beatrix of the Netherlands, Princess Grace of Monaco, the 350-pound King of Tonga and—royal in demeanor, anyway—First Lady Nancy Reagan, officially representing the U.S.) to the dramatic procession along the 652-foot red carpet at St. Paul's. Even Diana's brief verbal stumble—calling her groom Philip Charles Arthur George instead of Charles Philip Arthur George—seemed charming and momentarily transformed a grand state occasion into a real wedding with real people. Charles flubbed his lines as well, promising to share "all my goods" instead of "all my worldly goods." But on that magical July morning, failure seemed impossible. Like everyone else, the bride was bewitched. "I had," she said later, "tremendous hopes in my heart." If Diana's fans believed in happily ever after, well, once upon a time, she did too.

**EYES ON THE PRIZE** "We do this sort of thing rather well," said Charles (bending gallantly toward his bride at Buckingham Palace). He wore his Royal Navy commander's uniform; she, 40 yards of silk from Lullingstone, England's only silkworm farm.

# UPON A TIME

For one shining moment, the Waleses transfixed the world with their happiness as they exchanged vows

**BACKSTAGE**
Di barely knew attendants India Hicks and Sarah Jane Gaselee (left and center), but little Clementine Hambro had been her pupil.

**GRAND ASCENT** Diana's
25-foot train was badly wrinkled
because the designers hadn't
realized it would get bunched
up inside the Glass Coach.

**THE LONG WALK** Diana's father was recovering from a stroke, and she worried he might not be strong enough to stay by her side. "It was a deeply moving moment for us when he made it," her brother Charles said later.

**H**ere was a fairy story
that everybody wanted to work,'
Di told the BBC. 'At the age of 19,
you think you're prepared for
everything, and you think you
have the knowledge of what's
coming ahead'

———

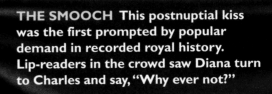

**THE SMOOCH** This postnuptial kiss was the first prompted by popular demand in recorded royal history. Lip-readers in the crowd saw Diana turn to Charles and say, "Why ever not?"

## STAMP ACT
At the photo session, Charles—like Di, 5'10"—stood on a box to make him seem taller. For 10 years she wore low heels.

## CANDID CAMERA
After weeks of tension preparing for the wedding of the century, the members of the bridal party collapsed with laughter as a photographer tried to capture the moment. The cast: five bridesmaids, two page boys and (top left) Charles's brothers Princes Andrew and Edward.

overleaf:
## OH, BROTHERS!
Using a lipstick borrowed from a lady-in-waiting, Andrew and Edward graced the honeymoon carriage with a superfluous sign and tri-plumed Prince of Wales balloons, echoed in Diana's John Boyd hat.

# WALES TO WOE

## They were opposites who attracted ceaseless attention to their misery

For all their wealth and privilege, they were just too far apart—in years, temperaments, expectations. She came from an emotional, fragmented family; he from a coldly dutiful one. He kept largely to his intellectual and aristocratic pursuits. She, dumped in the gilded fishbowl without a guide, found her own way. "We both made mistakes," Diana would admit. How could they not? They were trapped—by his devotion to an old flame, by her resentment of a "crowded" marriage that involved three, by his fear of losing the crown, by her terror of losing her children. And certainly, the world's fascination played a part. "We didn't want to disappoint the public," Diana said in her 1995 BBC interview. She was thus left with a "deep, profound" sadness. "The fairy tale," she said, "had ended."

**DEVOLUTION In retrospect, official portraits by Lord Snowdon (top row: 1981; bottom row: left, 1985; right, 1991) couldn't fully disguise the increasing strain at the union's core.**

**LIP SERVICE** Although Diana
was never a big polo fan, she publicly
cheered Charles on, encouraging him
after a loss at Cirencester Park in 1985
(top) and presenting him with a silver
cup after a win at Windsor in 1988.

**TUG OF WILLS** For a week between his birth and his August 1982 christening, Prince William went unnamed while Charles lobbied for the appellation "Arthur." Di won. The Queen expressed relief that "he hasn't got ears like his father."

# The emotional gap between them widened to become an unbridgeable gulf

**BACK TALK** Diana was seven months pregnant and, according to author Andrew Morton, had already hurled herself down the stairs once in a fit of despair when she hotly drove Charles away from a 1982 polo match.

LIONEL CHERRUAULT (2)

# Not all the pain and heartache could be laid at Charles's feet

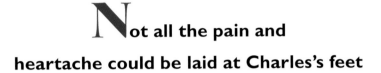

**IN MOURNING** Diana found one of her few early allies in bodyguard Graham Smith, who died of cancer in 1993. She skipped public duties to attend his funeral.

**DARLING DADDY** In Austria when her father, Lord Spencer, died of a heart attack in 1992, Diana flew home for the service and pinned a note (top) to a wreath.

**STITCHED** Di brought Wills home in 1991 after surgery on his forehead following an accidental beaning with a golf club. She had stayed with him in the hospital. Charles visited en route to the opera.

Charles and Camilla
Parker Bowles (in 1996)
shared a passion for
riding, country life and
each other. She vetted
all his girlfriends and,
after his marriage,
frequently served as his
hostess at Highgrove
instead of Di

# Before and after Di, Camilla was
## the mainstay of Charles's emotional life

**WITH FRIENDS LIKE THESE** Newly dating
Charles, Di was approached by Camilla
(with Di at one of the prince's horse races at
Ludlow in October 1980) in an unsuccessful attempt
to befriend her. Diana was correctly suspicious.

# Diana found her own solace, with friends and at least one lover

**LOVING CUP** Diana and James Hewitt (facing page) had been having an affair three years when she (with Wills) handed him a trophy in 1991. In 1996 the estranged wife of rugby star Will Carling (top, with Di at right) claimed he had privately admitted being Di's lover. Di denied it; so did Carling, calling her "a good friend." In 1994, Di's art dealer friend Oliver Hoare (above left) had police trace silent phone calls to his house. Ten came from Kensington Palace. In her '89 phone chats with James Gilbey (above right, with a 1994 date), Di was "Squidgy" and "Darling."

**PAST PRETENDING**
All the jewels and pomp could not hide Diana's misery during her last overseas trip with Charles, to Korea in November 1992. They fought, stood back-to-back and could barely disguise their rancor. In December, they separated.

TIM GRAHAM/SYGMA

**IN TRANSITION**
Di (leaving a London
restaurant in February
1996, three weeks
before agreeing to
the divorce) wore
a plain gold band in
place of her famous
engagement ring—
but with its matching
earrings still winking.

**P**ost-divorce, Diana found support and stability through an international network of friends, some famous themselves

### PALS IN NEED
She comforted Elton John, who wept inconsolably at the July funeral for their friend Gianni Versace in Milan's Duomo. Just before her own death, Diana and the singer had made up following a tiff over her withdrawal from a book party for the designer. The princess was a forgiver who could never forget her chums. As John sang at her service, "All our words cannot express the joy you brought us through the years..."

# **D**odi seemed suited to Di, like her
# a privileged outsider with a sensitive soul

**LAST LOVE** Diana first met Dodi Al Fayed in 1986, when his father Mohammed's polo team, for which Dodi played, beat Charles's team at Windsor Great Park. The romance did not bloom, however, until July 1997, when the elder Fayed, the Egyptian-born owner of Harrods, invited Di and her sons to vacation with his family at his Saint-Tropez villa. Onboard the Fayed yacht (top) Di and Dodi discovered they were kindred spirits. After two more Riviera retreats together, the lovers arrived in Paris on August 30 (above). That day, he gave her a $205,000 diamond ring. She had given him cuff links belonging to her late father.

**JOURNEY'S END** On their final evening, Di and Dodi dined at the Paris Ritz, owned by his father, then dispatched their driver to decoy the oppressive paparazzi. Henri Paul, a security officer of the hotel, later determined to have imbibed thrice the legal alcohol limit, was summoned to chauffeur the couple. Another Ritz staffer (left) watched, as she entered a Mercedes S-280, behind Dodi's bodyguard, Trevor Rees-Jones. Speeding to elude the press, the car careened into a support column of a Seine-side tunnel and crumpled. Rees-Jones was the sole survivor.

# SHE COULD HAVE

On a magical
evening in 1985,
Diana proved to
be one singular
sensation

**A**s a child, Diana hoped to be a ballerina. That dream was tabled in her teens, when she reached her full height of 5'10"—too tall to be a classical danseuse. But in October 1985 she asked well-known British dancer Wayne Sleep to choreograph a routine for her to perform at the Christmas benefit for the Friends of Covent Garden at the Royal Opera House. It was to be "a surprise for her husband," Sleep says. Diana chose Billy Joel's "Uptown Girl," one of her favorite songs, and secretly trained a few hours a week at various studios.

During the first two-thirds of the benefit Diana sat beside Charles. Then she quietly left the royal box, slipped out of her red velvet dress and changed into a clingy, cream-satin gown.

Sleep was first onstage. "There was a big round of applause," he recalls, "and I thought, 'Oh, you ain't seen nothing yet.'" Indeed, the crowd gasped when Diana made her entrance. "I told her to

walk on for eight counts and then stand for eight more, because they are not going to believe it," Sleep says. "Every step we took was followed by a huge round of applause."

But Diana seemed to be performing for an audience of one—her stunned husband, whose box was right over the stage. Diana's routine was "among the most provocative and sensuous pieces of theater you are ever going to see," recalls Reg Wilson, Covent Garden's official photographer that evening. "She kept looking up at Charles. There was an enormous sense of fun between the two of them. . . . He was very happy and smiling the whole time."

At the end of the 4-minute routine, the duo took eight curtain calls, and Diana begged for a reprise. "I said no," says Sleep, "because then they would start nitpicking. She's a good dancer, but she isn't a professional. She started to do it again, and I had to drag her off. She loved it."

**STAR TURN** Diana was nervous when she first came onstage, but she soon relaxed. "I lifted her across the stage, and then she would kick over my head," says Sleep, her 5'1" partner. "It was comical because, obviously, she towered over me." Says photographer Reg Wilson: "I think Charles was surprised by what she could do, because she was dancing extremely well. He wasn't embarrassed. He just blushed an awful lot."

# HANDS-ON MOM

## William and Harry were the most important men in Diana's life

Diana was 6 the first time her world fell apart. In 1967 her mother, Frances, left her father, Earl Spencer, for another man. Having unhappily shuttled between her mother's London townhouse and her father's country estates, trying to please two stepparents, Diana vowed to give her sons real nurturing. She appears to have done just that—despite unique pressures. "I admired and respected her," the Queen eulogized Diana, "especially for her devotion to her two boys."

Although both William and Harry had nannies from birth, Diana breast-fed her sons and remained a devoted mum to the end. She and her boys rode roller coasters, shot rapids, took in movies and visited burger joints. Diana insisted they attend a regular school—rather than receive tutoring by a governess, as Charles had—to learn something about the real world. As they grew, her task became more complex, particularly with William, the handsome 6'1" heir to the throne who was, at 15, already being cast as a global teen idol. Even as she encouraged him to take on more royal duties, such as walkabouts and reviewing parades, she instructed, "Lead from the heart, not the head." Toward that end, she took her sons to visit AIDS patients and homeless shelters to better understand what she called "people's emotions, insecurities, distress and hopes and dreams."

She taught her boys well. It was William who persuaded the divorced Diana to auction off her royal frocks to raise funds for charity. And it was William who insisted that both sons attend their mother's casket the final mile of the funeral procession. Ahead of his Windsor elders, the future king seemed to grasp the popular claim on Diana's memory.

**WINSOME SMILES In 1988, William, then 6, Harry, almost 4, and Diana posed for a portrait at Highgrove as a 40th-birthday present for Charles.**

**HOT TODDLER** After 18-month-old William posed with his parents (above), stores carrying his snowsuit sold out.

**RED ALERT** Charles and Diana looked like proud parents (left) when they brought Harry home from the hospital in September 1984, but Diana told friends that Charles had wanted a girl and complained about Harry's "rusty hair."

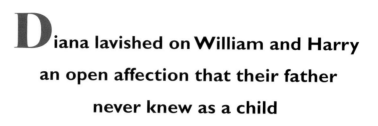

# **D**iana lavished on William and Harry an open affection that their father never knew as a child

**PUTTING IT TOGETHER**
In 1985, Diana, the former nursery
school aide, helped William, then 3,
with a puzzle at Kensington Palace.
An excellent student, William
was able to read at 5.

**A LEG UP** Diana looked after Harry, 3, and William, 5, during a 1987 holiday in Spain, where they were guests of the Spanish royal family. Charles was behind Di on the steps of Marivent Palace, near Palma, Majorca.

**EMBRACEABLE YOUS** Wills and Harry got a royal welcome
during the family's visit to Toronto in October 1991.

**GUTSY CALL** Diana thought she had won the mothers' race at
Wills's school in 1989, but judges declared her second.

**THE NEW KID**
William, 7, and Di stood by as Harry, 5, arrived for his first day at London's Wetherby pre-prep school in 1989. An average student, Harry looks up to William, who has kept a watchful eye on him.

**STRIDE RIGHT Diana and Harry, 7, set out for the slopes in Lech, Austria, in 1992. Charles joined the family a few days later.**

**DIGGING DI** On Necker Island in the Caribbean, William, 7, and Harry, 5, covered Mum with the help of their cousins.

**ALL ABOARD** On a school vacation in 1994, Diana held on to Harry, 9, as William, 11, and their pals rode the roller coaster at Alton Towers, a Staffordshire amusement park.

**D**espite the confines of her position, Diana
tried to have fun with her sons just like any other mother

**ROYAL ROOTERS** Di shared her joy with William as Steffi Graf beat Gabriela Sabatini
in the 1991 Wimbledon women's final. They were pulling for Graf, who had played doubles
with Diana and had offered Wills private instruction.

**COAST CLEAR?**
While she understood press and public fascination with the young princes, Diana (peeking from a Knightsbridge eatery with Harry in 1994) tried to limit their exposure.

**SPLASHDANCE** Diana updated the traditional watering holes of the wealthy, and in July 1997, she let Wills run circles around her on the Riviera. They and Harry were guests of Dodi Al Fayed at his father's villa.

**SEA CHANGE** That same month at St. Tropez, 16 summers after her honeymoon, which had also been on the Mediterranean, she gave Harry a loving hug. It turned out to be the last vacation that Mummy would share with her sons.

**HIGHLAND HIKE As always in August, the princes wound down their 1997 summer vacation at Balmoral. Two weeks after walking with Charles to a waterfall on the royal grounds, their mother died.**

**ABOVE IT ALL** In 1991, Di climbed 220 steps to Rio's Christ the Redeemer statue for a bird's-eye view of the city and an official earful.

# MAGIC TOUCH

As England's goodwill ambassador, Diana offered a warm smile, a ready ear and a natural empathy that enabled her to connect with people like few royals before her

Cuddling babies, inspecting troops, even driving a tank: For Princess Diana it was all in a day's work. The most popular member of the royal family, she was also often the busiest, logging thousands of hours and air miles each year to visit the sick and elderly, and raise funds for more than 100 charities. (Her presence at a benefit could double an evening's take.) But Diana didn't do it for the adulation. Herself a child of a broken home, she brought to the job an empathic disposition that complemented her aristocratic pedigree. "I think the biggest disease this world suffers from in this day and age is the disease of people feeling unloved," she said in 1995. "I know I can give love." Indeed, Di always seemed to go the extra kilometer, learning sign language to address a deaf association and penning personal notes to the families of hospital patients she had met. While many people shunned AIDS patients and lepers, the princess literally embraced them, as she did the homeless, battered and drug-addicted. During her last year, Diana traveled to Bosnia and Angola to press her campaign for a ban on land mines. She also auctioned off 79 evening gowns to raise $5.76 million for AIDS and breast-cancer charities. "People think that at the end of the day a man is the only answer," Diana once said. "Actually, a fulfilling job is better for me."

**ROYAL RUB** Touring New Zealand with Charles in 1983,
Diana charmed well-wishers by adopting the traditional greeting
of the Maori people: the hongi, or nose press.

**CONNECTING**
Diana's engaging
smile and natural
warmth made her
an ambassador
worth her weight in
ermine and tiaras.
On one 1991 visit
to a Somerset,
England, center for
the disabled, a
handshake turned
into an ecstatic
clasp.

## NOT IMMUNE

The first Windsor to focus public attention on **AIDS**, Diana buoyed patients in a London **AIDS** ward in 1989 (right) and held **HIV**-positive children (below) in Brazil in 1991. "It's heartbreaking," she said. After separating from Charles in 1992, she focussed on a select handful of issues, among them breast cancer and land-mine devastation.

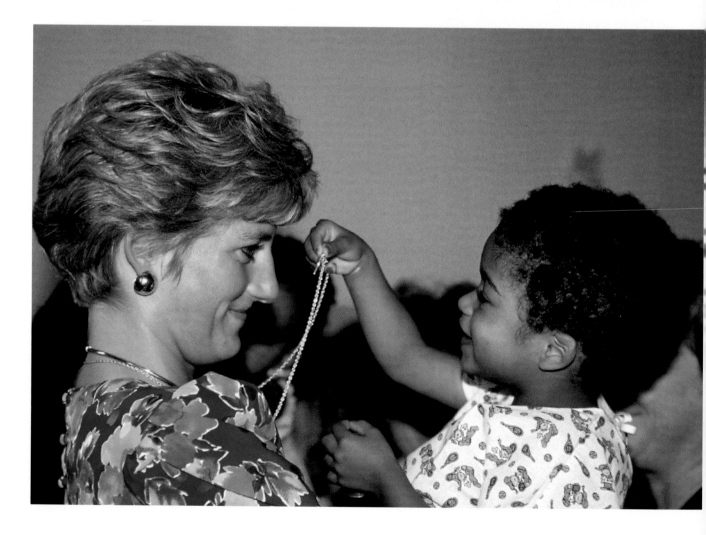

## SHE ALWAYS MADE A SPLASH

In 1990 (above) the unpretentious princess stooped to conquer a class of disabled swimmers at an Ipswich, England, pool. "She has a keen sense of humor and puts people at ease," a charity director once said. During a 1992 tour of India the princess traveled to Mother Teresa's Calcutta mission (right), where she praised the nuns' efforts to help the poor. "I think you are terrific," Di told them. "You bring light to people's lives." Ironically, Mother Teresa passed away five days after Diana's death.

**TABLE TALK** When Diana was in the U.S. for a breast cancer fund-raiser in 1996, Hillary Clinton arranged a White House power breakfast for her to meet other movers in the philanthropic world.

**MUTUAL ADMIRERS** South African president Nelson Mandela welcomed her to Cape Town in March, 1997, to discuss the threat of AIDS. "It's not often that I meet princesses," said Mandela, praising her effort to reduce prejudice against AIDS patients. "I'm still trembling."

**CRUSADER** During a January 1997, Red Cross mission to Angola, Diana visited a rehabilitation center to comfort victims of the nation's devastating 20-year civil war. "That was very traumatic, as a mother, to witness," she told the **BBC**, raising consciousness worldwide on land mines and propelling the signing of a 100-nation treaty outlawing their use.

WHEN IN PAKISTAN Visiting a mosque in Lahore in 1993, Diana donned a gold-embroidered shawl in accordance with Muslim tradition.

# No matter how awkward the occasion, Diana charmed her audience with an easy tandem of good looks and good humor

**AB FAB**
A blushing Diana couldn't help but grin
as she bestowed an award on a team of lifeguards
during her 1988 Australia visit. The lifeguards had wanted
to wear track suits, but photographers persuaded
them to stay in uniform.

**TANK TOP** Fetching even in army "denims," Di slipped through the hatch of an armored vehicle for a rumbling tour of Hampshire's Tidworth army barracks in 1988.

**SWEET DREAM** It was a tiring (and sometimes tiresome) job, but when Di nodded off at a 1981 gala, the reason, undisclosed at the time, was that she was pregnant with Wills.

In transforming herself from novice to knockout, Diana demonstrated that 'British style' was no oxymoron

# DIVA

**DETAILING**
Diana made little things count, like glittering buttons on a satin evening jacket (left). Once dotty for spots, she renounced polka-dot power after 1987 (center). Though she grew to favor neutral shoes, Di once loved whimsical footwear.

OF STYLE

# Once Diana ditched the fuddy-duddy Windsor duds, she discovered her own sexy sleekness

She entered the marriage with jeans, a few cashmere sweaters and one long dress, plus a collection of Laura Ashley dirndls that were the Sloane Ranger uniform. Only six years later, the Princess of Wales owned more than 80 suits, 12-dozen evening gowns and 50 day dresses, plus matching shoes and clutches galore. Two meticulous women dressers labored full-time to keep it all cleaned, sorted and cataloged. With the early guidance of pals at British Vogue, she educated her eye and became, in time, a style setter: When Di donned polka-dot socks, they sold out nationwide. The day the astrakhan muff appeared in 1981, Harrods was stormed. Her example helped to popularize the ruffled collar, the pearl choker and the smart suit for everyday. Her worth to the British fashion industry was estimated in the tens of millions. Appropriately, several fashion luminaries, including Valentino, Donatella Versace and Karl Lagerfeld, were on hand to pay their respects at her funeral.

### BUSY BODY
At first, Diana came off a tad frumpy in candy stripes (at Ascot in 1981, above left) and in a loud print for a 1983 visit to London's Royal Academy (left). By 1985 she had developed a more tailored look, thanks partly to Catherine Walker.

### STREAMLINED
Trim and bright was the suit slogan in 1995. The tangerine Catherine Walker (right) wowed Liverpool; the pink Versace (center) starred in Buenos Aires. For Christmas 1994, faux fur, ankle boots and a pew-perfect slit skirt got her to the church on time.

## DI AFTER DARK:
Year after year she 'consistently amazed,' wrote fashion editor Sue James

**OUT ON THE GOWN**
(left to right) Di went dramatic at a 1995 Manhattan fashion fete where her friend Liz Tilberis, editor of *Harper's Bazaar*, was an honoree. She was classic, in turquoise, for a 1988 state dinner in London. Diana showed shoulders in a white gown at Cannes in 1987. In the sexy black Stambolian she wore in June 1994, Di bid to upstage Charles the night he admitted adultery on TV. A scarlet Victor Edelstein enhanced a 1991 arrival.

### A TAD SHEEPISH
A British company sold $1 million worth of the lamb-lineup sweater (center left, in 1983) after Di was photographed wearing it. As for that year's clamdiggers (far left), nobody shelled out.

### COWBOY MOM
Striding into Wetherby school in 1989 (near left) called for a certain swagger. And where else in the course of a royal day could she flaunt those cool boots?

### PUMP AND RUN
To dash to and from the health club (top right, in July 1997), Di often threw on a big sweatshirt over bike shorts. Di adored things American.

### BLADE RUNNER
Even a quick spin around Kensington Gardens in 1995 (right) meant shorts to match one of her new fave baseball caps, perfect for the pre-hairdresser hours.

# **B**eing Diana meant (almost) never having a bad hair day

'81 '82 '83 '84 '84 '85 '85 '87 '87 '88 '89 '90 '91 '94 '95 '96

**CHANGING LOCKS** The schoolgirl look (1981) was jettisoned, but the mid-'80s tucks and twists brought cries of dowdiness from the British tabs. Di's 1991 crop was called a sign of sexual rebellion. Although she spent an estimated $14,000 a year on hair care, a stiff breeze could blow it all (1982).

(ABOVE) LIONEL CHERRUAULT (2); JAYNE FINCHER/PHOTOGRAPHERS INTERNATIONAL (10); TIM GRAHAM/SYGMA (2); NUNN SYNDICATION; TIM ROOKE/REX USA; (RIGHT) LIONEL CHERRUAULT

**COMPLEMENTARY**
On a trip to Australia in late 1985, Diana won raves in an elegant black-and-white Bruce Oldfield suit at the Melbourne Cup races.

**HEADS UP** The chapeaux must go on for all royal ladies, but it took Diana to make them fun. And ubiquitous. By 1989, she owned about 75.

# AT PEACE

As captivating for her flaws as for her glamour, Diana remains an intriguing riddle

**M**agical in life, tragic in death, the People's Princess has entered the realm of myth. Paradoxically, even as admirers exalt Diana, it was her flaws and vulnerabilities that made her the most widely loved royal of all time. Her special gift was for making the people she met feel special. "Everyone needs to be valued," she once said. And therein lay her true magic: Though we never knew Diana, she made us believe she knew us.

**HOMECOMING** Flowers left at the Althorp gate were rowed to the island where **Diana** is buried.

"Above all, we give thanks
for the life of a woman
I am so proud to be able
to call my sister:
the unique, the complex,
the extraordinary and
irreplaceable Diana,
whose beauty, both
internal and external,
will never be extinguished
from our minds."

— EARL SPENCER

# INDEX